BLACK

ACHIEVEMENTS

IN SPORTS

CELEBRATING FRITZ POLLARD, SIMONE BILES, AND MORE

ELLIOTT SMITH
CICELY LEWIS, EXECUTIVE EDITOR

Lerner Publications ◆ Minneapolis

LETTER FROM CICELY LEWIS

Dear Reader,

As a girl, I wanted to be like Oprah Winfrey. She is a Black woman from Mississippi like me who became an award-winning actor, author, and businessperson. Oftentimes, history books leave out the accomplishments and contributions of people of color. When you

CICELY LEWIS

see someone who looks like you and has a similar background excelling at something, it helps you to see yourself be great.

I created Read Woke to amplify the voices of people who are often underrepresented. These books bring to light the beauty, talent, and integrity of Black people in music, activism, sports, the arts, and other areas. As you read, think about why it's important to celebrate Black excellence and the achievements of all people regardless of race, gender, or status. How did the people mentioned succeed despite barriers placed on them? How can we use these stories to inspire others?

Black excellence is everywhere in your daily life. I hope these people inspire you to never give up and continue to let your light shine.

With gratitude,

Cicely Lewis

TABLE OF CONTENTS

SPEED RACER

For nearly twenty years, Allyson Felix blazed around the track, setting multiple track-and-field records. Felix specialized in the 200-meter sprint. She also ran on several US relay teams.

Fast and consistent, Felix is the most decorated US track and-field athlete in the history of the Olympic Games. She has eleven Olympic medals, including seven gold. And she won nineteen World Championship medals. She also advocates for women's rights. When Nike, the shoe company that sponsored her, revealed it would pay her 70 percent less when she became pregnant, Felix left the brand. Later, she started her own shoe company, Saysh.

This book explores Black excellence in sports. While not every groundbreaking athlete is in this title, the ones highlighted have helped shape or innovate their sports and inspire the next generation of athletes.

Felix runs in the 200-meter race at the 2004 Olympics. She won the silver medal.

Tennis star Althea Gibson kisses her 1956 French Open trophy.

CHAPTER 1

PIONEERS

Black athletes overcame segregation and racism to succeed in sports. The road was hard for these groundbreakers. But their successes showed Black athletes were here to stay.

THE PLAYER-COACH

Fritz Pollard was a superstar college football player at Brown. The running back led Brown to the 1916 Rose Bowl. But there weren't many roads to pro football for Black players then. In 1919 Pollard joined the Akron Pros, making him the first Black player in what would become the National Football League (NFL).

With Pollard in the backfield, the Pros went undefeated and won the league championship. In 1921 Pollard became the team's co-coach. He was the first and only Black head coach until 1988. Pollard joined the Pro Football Hall of Fame in 2005.

Fritz Pollard posing with a football in 1916

DID YOU KNOW?

Willie O'Ree was the first Black player in the National Hockey League. The Boston Bruins retired his jersey number, 22, in 2022 to honor his career.

GRAND CHAMPION

Althea Gibson was among the best tennis players of her day. But racism made it difficult to showcase her talents. White-only clubs refused to let her play there, and tournaments often claimed they lost her event applications. But in 1951, Gibson became the first Black player at Wimbledon.

Gibson then became the first Black player to win a Grand Slam at the 1956 French Open. It was the first of her eleven Grand Slam titles, including the 1957 Wimbledon crown. Queen Elizabeth II presented the trophy. After her tennis career ended, Gibson played professional golf.

REFLECT

How would you feel if you weren't allowed to play the sport you loved? Why do you think Gibson and other pioneers kept pushing to play?

Gibson crouches to hit the ball during a 1951 match.

AGELESS ARM

Leroy "Satchel" Paige was a first-rate baseball pitcher. He threw many unique pitches. Sometimes he made infielders sit while he struck out hitters. He was a star in the Negro Leagues but couldn't join Major League Baseball (MLB) because they didn't allow Black players.

When Jackie Robinson broke the color line in 1947, Paige was ready to show his stuff. He joined MLB in 1948 at the age of forty-two, becoming the oldest player to ever join MLB. Paige became the first Black player to pitch in the World Series, helping Cleveland win in 1948. And Paige pitched in his final MLB game at fifty-nine, making him the oldest player in MLB history.

Leroy "Satchel" Paige around 1940

"Age is a question of mind over matter. If you don't mind, it doesn't matter."

—Satchel Paige

Paige warms up to pitch. He helped the Cleveland team win many games.

Celebrated boxer Muhammad Ali fights in a 1962 match.

CHAPTER 2

REVOLUTIONARIES

Many people love athletes for their skills and performance. But athletes are people too, and they have concerns about the world they live in. Many Black athletes fight for civil rights and economic justice. Their powerful roles as public figures help create change.

THE GREATEST

Many believe Muhammad Ali is the greatest boxer of all time. But he was also a man with firm beliefs. He felt strongly about his Islamic faith. He changed his name from Cassius Clay to Muhammad Ali. He stood by his name even as others refused to use it.

Ali opposed the Vietnam War (1955–1975). When he refused to join the army in 1967, he was stripped of his heavyweight championship title. Ali did not box for three years. But he still spoke out against the war whenever he could. More people began to agree with him. When he began to box again, Ali became a hero and champion once more.

Ali (*left*) could block many different hits.

SEEKING JUSTICE

Maya Moore was an all-star player for the Minnesota Lynx in the Women's National Basketball Association. But she left the sport in 2019. She faced a bigger challenge—reforming the US prison and criminal justice system. Moore began work in 2016 to free Jonathan Irons from a wrongful conviction.

Moore used her voice to draw attention to Irons and other, mostly Black prisoners who have been wrongly imprisoned or harshly sentenced. In July 2020, Irons was freed after twenty-three years in prison. Moore continues to speak out against injustice. For now, basketball is on hold.

Maya Moore (*left*) with Jonathan Irons a year after she helped free him from prison

TAKING A KNEE

The protest that shook sports started small. In 2016 few noticed during the first three 49ers preseason games that Colin Kaepernick sat during the national anthem. After talking to a teammate, Kaepernick took a knee during the next game in protest. The quarterback explained his protest was about bringing awareness to police brutality and social injustice.

> "I love America. I love people. That's why I'm doing this. I want to help make America better."
> —COLIN KAEPERNICK, FORMER 49ERS QUARTERBACK, IN 2016

Teammates such as Eric Reid (*left*) kneeled with Colin Kaepernick during some games.

Kaepernick took a knee throughout that season. Other players joined him. Critics urged the quarterback to stick to sports. But Kaepernick continued, even at the cost of his career. Kaepernick has not played in the NFL since 2017. Some people believe he hasn't been signed by a team because of his protests. But Kaepernick helped change the conversation around athletes and activism.

Kaepernick receiving the Muhammad Ali Legacy Award, which celebrates an athlete's sportsmanship, in 2017

REFLECT

Should athletes speak out against injustice? How might speaking out affect fans or other athletes?

Basketball legend LeBron James leaps for a basket.

CHAPTER 3

THE G.O.A.T.s

These athletes are the best of the best. It takes talent and passion to reach the top, and these Black superstars have become legends. Many consider them the greatest of all time in their sports.

AIR JORDAN

Michael Jordan's dunks were legendary. His ability to score anytime was unmatched. He was one of the most clutch players in National Basketball Association (NBA) history. Winning six NBA titles with the Chicago Bulls and scoring more than thirty thousand points in his career, Jordan was one of the greatest basketball players ever. Players still imitate his style and swagger.

Jordan also scored off the court. His work with Nike changed the sneaker business. He starred in the hit movie *Space Jam*. And he's a majority owner of the Charlotte Hornets. His success is impressive for a player who didn't make the varsity basketball team as a high school sophomore.

Michael Jordan hangs off the rim and cheers after a dunk.

DID YOU KNOW?

LeBron James is on pace to become the NBA's all-time leading scorer. Entering the 2022–2023 season, he had 37,062 points. Kareem Abdul-Jabbar is first with 38,387.

Kareem Abdul-Jabbar avoids a block to aim for a basket.

QUEEN OF THE COURT

Serena Williams's father taught Serena and her sister Venus to play tennis on cracked courts in Compton, California. Very few Black athletes were playing tennis. The sisters faced racism. Venus became famous first, but Serena helped change the game.

Serena Williams is one of the best players in modern tennis. Using an amazing mix of power, speed, and skill, Williams has captured twenty-three Grand Slam singles titles and four Olympic gold medals. She has battled racism and sexism but never hesitates to speak out or help other players.

Left to right: Serena and Venus Williams compete in a doubles match at the 2018 French Open.

GRACE UNDER PRESSURE

Simone Biles's gymnastics skills are legendary. She has seven Olympic medals, tied for the most of any American gymnast. And she has twenty-five World Championship medals, the most of any gymnast worldwide. Four gymnastics moves are named after her.

In the 2020 Tokyo Olympics, held in 2021 due to COVID-19, Biles was the favorite to win the all-around title. But the pressure made things difficult. Biles needed to step back. By focusing on her mental and physical health, she helped other athletes realize that taking a break is important. Biles returned for the balance beam final and won the bronze medal.

Simone Biles shows her gravity-defying moves during the 2019 World Championships.

REFLECT

Why do you think it is important for elite athletes to take mental health breaks?

Biles won bronze for her balance beam performance at the 2020 Tokyo Olympics.

Simone Manuel slicing through the water during the 50-meter freestyle semifinals at the 2019 World Championships

CHAPTER 4

NEXT-GENERATION STARS

New sports stars always find a way to shine. The latest generation of Black athletes breaks barriers in many sports and proves there's no sport that isn't open for everyone.

SERVING NOTICE

At just fifteen years old, Coco Gauff had the tennis world buzzing with what reporters called Cocomania. She qualified for Wimbledon in 2019 and made it to the fourth round. Gauff plays as though she had decades of experience. Grand Slam victories are on the horizon for this tennis prodigy.

Gauff started playing tennis when she was about seven years old. Her idols were the Williams sisters. She started entering junior tournaments and climbed the ranks. She reached the French Open final in 2022 and was in the top 15 of the Women's Tennis Association rankings.

Coco Gauff swinging during Wimbledon in 2019

DID YOU KNOW?

In 2015 Blake Bolden was the first Black player in the National Women's Hockey League. The league later changed its name to the Premier Hockey Federation. In 2020 she became a scout for the National Hockey League's Los Angeles Kings. She's the second woman to ever be a scout in the league.

TACKLING BARRIERS

Most people consider football to be a men's sport. But that didn't stop Adrienne Smith. Smith was just seven years old when her father taught her how to throw a football in a perfect spiral. In 2006 she joined the New York Sharks as a professional football player.

Smith shines on the field. In 2010 she became a member of the first US National Women's Football Team. She scored the first-ever touchdown in the history of women's international tackle football at the International Federation of American Football's Women's World Championship in Sweden that year. The US team took home gold. Smith has also won four Women's Football Alliance national championships. Her career inspires other women and girls to try football.

FREESTYLE FLASH

Often Black athletes don't get the opportunity to shine in certain sports such as swimming. Simone Manuel shattered stereotypes. During the 2016 Rio Olympics, Manuel became the first Black woman to win an individual gold medal in swimming. She won gold in the 100-meter freestyle.

Manuel continued to excel in the 50-meter and 100-meter freestyle. She won both events at the 2019 World Championships, becoming the first American woman to win both events at one World Championship. Manuel is also an ambassador for swimming. Her goal is to get more Black athletes involved in swimming to make the sport more diverse.

Manuel swims in the semifinals before winning Olympic gold in the 100-meter freestyle in 2016.

REFLECT

Think about the last time you tried a new sport. Were you nervous or scared? How did you overcome it and have fun?

Black athletes have overcome difficult challenges to excel in sports. They've opened the door for other athletes to explore new sports too. As Black athletes make strides in sports like cricket and curling, the tradition of Black excellence continues. Explore new sports and discover the Black athletes starring in their fields.

Coco Gauff and other Black athletes continue to transform their sports.

GLOSSARY

activism: the belief or practice of trying to make social change through action

ambassador: a representative or messenger

clutch: something done well in an important situation

conviction: being found guilty of doing something, often a crime

Grand Slam: one of the four major tournaments in pro tennis, including the Australian Open, the French Open, Wimbledon (in England), and the US Open

prodigy: a young child who has great ability in something

scout: a person who looks for talented athletes

segregation: the practice of separating people because of their race

stereotype: an idea, often untrue, about a certain person or group

SOURCE NOTES

10   "Satchel Paige," National Baseball Hall of Fame, accessed July 6, 2022, https://baseballhall.org/hall-of-famers/paige-satchel.

15   Cindy Boren, "A Timeline of Colin Kaepernick's Protests against Police Brutality, Four Years after They Began," *Washington Post*, August 26, 2020, https://www.washingtonpost.com/sports /2020/06/01/colin-kaepernick-kneeling-history/.

READ WOKE READING LIST

Adrienne Smith
https://www.bostonrenegadesfootball.org/player/smith
-adrienne/

Braun, Eric. *Colin Kaepernick: From Free Agent to Change Agent*. Minneapolis: Lerner Publications, 2020.

Britannica Kids: Negro Leagues
https://kids.britannica.com/students/article/Negro-leagues
/632863

Lowell, Barbara. *Maya Moore*. Mankato, MN: Black Rabbit Books, 2020.

Morgan, Sally. *Simone Biles: Golden Girl of Gymnastics.* New York: Random House Children's Books, 2020.

National Museum of African American History & Culture: "Sports: Leveling the Playing Field"
https://nmaahc.si.edu/explore/exhibitions/sports

Smith, Elliott. *Serena Williams*. Minneapolis: Lerner Publications, 2021.

Sports Illustrated Kids: Coco Gauff
https://www.sikids.com/kid-reporter/kid-reporter-q-a-coco
-gauff

INDEX

PHOTO ACKNOWLEDGMENTS

Image credits: David Ramos/Getty Images, p. 4; Jamie Squire/Getty Images, p. 5; Bettmann/Getty Images, pp. 6, 9, 11; Pro Football Hall Of Fame/NFL, p. 7; Mark Rucker/Transcendental Graphics/Getty Images, p. 10; Stanley Weston/Getty Images, p. 12; Bettmann/Getty Images, p. 13; Bonnie Biess/FilmMagic for Backstage Creations/Getty Images, p. 14; Michael Zagaris/San Francisco 49ers/Getty Images, p. 15; Slaven Vlasic/Getty Images for Sports Illustrated, p. 16; Steph Chambers/Getty Images, p. 17; JEFF HAYNES/AFP/Getty Images, p. 18; Focus on Sport/Getty Images, p. 19; Mustafa Yalcin/Anadolu Agency/Getty Images, p. 20; Laurence Griffiths/Getty Images, p. 21; The Asahi Shimbun/Getty Images, p. 22; FRANCOIS-XAVIER MARIT/AFP/Getty Images, p. 23; ADRIAN DENNIS/AFP/Getty Images, p. 24; Aaron Ontiveroz/The Denver Post/Getty Images, p. 26; Antonio Borga/Eurasia Sport Images/Getty Images, p. 27.

Cover: Zheng Huansong/Xinhua/Alamy Live News (Simone Biles); Pro Football Hall of Fame/AP Images (Fritz Pollard).

Lerner Publications Company
An imprint of Lerner Publishing Group, Inc.
241 First Avenue North
Minneapolis, MN 55401 USA

For reading levels and more information, look up this title at www.lernerbooks.com.

Main body text set in Aptifer Sans LT Pro.
Typeface provided by Linotype AG.

Editor: Lauren Foley **Designer:** Kim Morales

Library of Congress Cataloging-in-Publication Data

Names: Smith, Elliott, 1976– author.
Title: Black achievements in sports : celebrating Fritz Pollard, Simone Biles, and more / Elliott Smith.
Description: Minneapolis : Lerner Publications, 2024. | Series: Black excellence project. Read woke books | Includes bibliographical references and index. | Audience: Ages 9–14 | Audience: Grades 4–6 | Summary: "Black athletes break records, fight for equality, and inspire the next generation of athletes. From Muhammad Ali to Coco Gauff, learn about Black sports stars and their achievements"— Provided by publisher.
Identifiers: LCCN 2022033895 (print) | LCCN 2022033896 (ebook) | ISBN 9781728486628 (library binding) | ISBN 9781728496382 (ebook)
Subjects: LCSH: African American athletes—History—Juvenile literature. | African American athletes—Biography—Juvenile literature.
Classification: LCC GV583 .S625 2024 (print) | LCC GV583 (ebook) | DDC 796.089/96073—dc23/eng/20220720

LC record available at https://lccn.loc.gov/2022033895
LC ebook record available at https://lccn.loc.gov/2022033896

Manufactured in the United States of America
1-52592-50766-12/21/2022